My First Adventures

MY FIRST TRIP ON AN
AIRPLANE

By Katie Kawa

Gareth Stevens
Publishing

Please visit our website, www.garethstevens.com. For a free color catalog of all our high-quality books, call toll free 1-800-542-2595 or fax 1-877-542-2596.

Library of Congress Cataloging-in-Publication Data

Kawa, Katie.
My first trip on an airplane / Katie Kawa.
    p. cm. — (My first adventures)
Includes index.
ISBN 978-1-4339-7297-3 (pbk.)
ISBN 978-1-4339-7298-0 (6-pack)
ISBN 978-1-4339-7296-6 (library binding)
1. Air travel—Juvenile literature. I. Title.
HE9787.K39 2013
387.7'42—dc23

                                    2011047931

First Edition

Published in 2013 by
Gareth Stevens Publishing
111 East 14th Street, Suite 349
New York, NY 10003

Copyright © 2013 Gareth Stevens Publishing

Editor: Katie Kawa
Designer: Andrea Davison-Bartolotta

All Illustrations by Planman Technologies, pp. 24 (ticket) vectormart/shutterstock.com.

Printed in the United States of America

CPSIA compliance information: Batch #CS12GS: For further information contact Gareth Stevens, New York, New York at 1-800-542-2595.

Contents

I am going to visit
my grandpa!
He lives far away.

I am taking an airplane
to see him.

7

My family and I go
to the airport. This is
where we get on
the airplane.

It is busy! We wait
in a long line.

We need tickets to get on the airplane. These show us where to sit.

13

A pilot flies the airplane.

15

We put on
our seat belts.
Then, the airplane
starts to fly!

17

I read on the airplane.
My sister takes a nap.

Then, the airplane lands. It goes back on the ground.

21

My grandpa is there
to meet us!

23

Words to Know

pilot

seat belt

tickets

Index

24